Mallets &Music

A Guide to Four Mallet Marimba

Dr. Mark Boseman

Layout and Design by Mark Boseman

Music used with permission from Michael Burritt, Ivan Trevino, Blake Tyson, Aaron Staebell, Elliot Cole, Robert Honstein, Jennifer Bellor, Drew Worden, Matthew Curlee, and Baljinder Sekhon

Acknowledgements

Laura & Oliver: This book is for you. Both of you have helped show me what is really important in life. Thank you for being with me on this journey that at times, seems like one crazy turn after another. You have been with me through all of the ups and downs. I can't wait to see where life takes us in the future. Hopefully it will include a less stressful bedtime routine. I love you both.

Jan and Jerry Boseman: Thank you for getting me that cardboard drum set from Sears for Christmas when I was two years old. Who knew that would turn out to be one of the most influential gifts of my life. Whether it was at home or spending my off days from school exploring the corners of your band room with a Welch's grape soda in hand, you have always been an example of how to accomplish your goals with hard work, humility, and honesty. I have nothing against any other instruments, but thank you for picking out the red drums with the cardboard heads. It only took three days to completely destroy them but it was enough to spark a life long passion.

Michael Burritt: Thank you for pushing me in ways that I couldn't have imagined. I am so grateful for the time and energy that you have given me over the years. Your teaching and leadership have shaped me as a musician and teacher in ways that you can't imagine. I'm also grateful for the incredible memories that have very little to do with percussion or music. The times in Mexico, Germany, and everywhere in between were some of the most memorable experiences to date. This book has your fingerprints all over it and wouldn't have been possible without your mentorship.

Chalon Ragsdale: Thank you for giving me an incredible start on the marimba. I'll never forget showing up to that first lesson. I talked about how much trouble I had playing the instrument and with reading music in general. I'll always remember how puzzled I was when you asked if I had ever played with four mallets. I couldn't have imagined where that first lesson would ultimately take me. This wouldn't have been possible without your guidance throughout the years.

Lovingly dedicated to the memory of "Uncle" John Sample.

A special thank you goes to Dr. Ronda Mains and the University of Arkansas Department of Music for allowing me the use of the Stella Boyle Smith Concert Hall to record all of the videos for this book.

About the Author

Dr. Mark Boseman is a percussionist who specializes in both contemporary solo percussion as well as contemporary chamber music. His performances encompass a variety of styles that range from standard orchestral repertoire and contemporary chamber music to popular music styles. In addition, Mark has performed with a wide variety of ensembles ranging from the Civic Orchestra of Chicago to small chamber groups.

Dr. Boseman is currently teaching percussion at the University of Arkansas. During his time at the Eastman School of Music, he established himself as an international performer and educator. This resulted in yearly residencies at the Kunitachi College of Music in Tokyo and the Showa Academy of Music in Yokohama, Japan. These residencies include performance, masterclasses and private lessons on a wide variety of instruments and musical styles. In 2010, he accompanied the Eastman Broadband on their tour of New York City, Mexico City and the Cervantino Arts Festival in Guanajuato, Mexico. Additionally, Dr. Boseman is a member of Scatter Percussion Collective. This percussion septet performs original repertoire that blends popular and classical styles to create a unique and original sound.

Dr. Boseman holds a Bachelor's degree in music education from the University of Arkansas, a Master's degree in music performance and literature from Northwestern University, and a Doctorate of Musical Arts in music performance and literature degree from the Eastman School of Music. He is also a recipient of the Eastman School of Music's prestigious performer's certificate. His teachers have included Michael Burritt, Chalon Ragsdale, Bill Cahn, James Ross, Charles Ross, Rich Thompson and Paul Wertico.

Table of Contents

Before We Get Started. . .

The Numbers

Mallets are ordered from lowest to highest. In the left hand and starting from the outside, you will number them 1 and 2. 3 and 4 start on the inside mallet in the right hand. Many composers will use this system in their music to suggest a sticking that may help with complex passages.

The Height

The height of the instrument should be at a comfortable position that allows you to play without having to reach up and over the bars or to lean over or reach down to play. A good, general height is at your belt line. Many instruments will have some sort of height adjustment system. If it doesn't, there are a few measures that you can take to have the instrument at the proper height. For taller players, you can either get bed risers from Wal-Mart or Bed, Bath and Beyond or you can cut PVC pipe to the desired length. Make sure that the PVC diameter is slightly smaller than the diameter of the wheels. If you aren't quite tall enough, you might look into a lift to stand on. Unfortunately, it can be a more difficult solution because of limited height options.

The Music

To say that I'm lucky to have a world class group of composers that were enthusiastic about being a part of this project is an enormous understatement. Each composer has a unique style that will present you with new challenges, ideas, and experiences. The solos have a range in difficulty that are suitable for beginners up through intermediate musicians. In addition, each solo is accompanied by a page of exercises which were pulled from the corresponding solo and are intended to help you with the techniques involved. They should be considered as a starting point. In order to avoid stagnation, explore ways to augment the exercises with different dynamics, keys, phrasings or completely new variations. Be as creative as possible. If you don't like the exercises, compose or improvise new ones that benefit your needs. No two people learn in the same way.

The Videos

Videos are placed throughout the book in the form of QR codes that can be scanned with any smartphone or tablet. The videos found in the early chapters discuss the material within, while the videos in the latter half contain a performance of each piece as well as a short discussion of techniques, musical elements, and practice strategies. It should be noted that the performances are captured in one, continuous take, and because of this there may be a few errant notes. It is my hope that you will see how musicianship and technique can work together to create something more than they could alone. Also, in real life, a perfect performance is extremely rare.

- IOS, ANDROID, WINDOWS QR SCANNER - *i-nigma* can be found in all app stores.

1

Getting Started with the Basics

   The Stevens technique uses a more vertical hand position than its two counterparts, the traditional and Burton grips. These techniques use a more traditional flat position that is modeled after the technique used to play with two mallets. Because of this vertical position, the grip can be uncomfortable for students who are used to playing snare drum or using two mallets. It's important to take your time and build good habits. As you're learning this grip, you may want to "normalize" what you're feeling; that is to say make slight adjustments with your fingers or hand position in order to make it more comfortable. Your hands may automatically want to turn inward to a flat position out of pure habit. It's also important to know that this is completely normal. Try not to confuse "new" with "too hard". Perhaps the best activity during this time is to simply hold the mallets as much as possible without playing. Spending time reading, studying or watching TV while holding the mallets will help your hands adjust to the new grip without the added burden of playing the instrument. Periodically look down to make sure that your hands haven't changed the grip in any way and continue your activity. This will not only allow your hands to adjust, but it can also develop the ability to focus on one thing and keep the grip in place. The ultimate goal is for your hands to automatically do what you want them to without constantly thinking about it.

   These step by step instructions, along with the accompanying pictures and videos, will give you an easy and straightforward description of how to begin using the Stevens technique. Since the grip is identical in each hand, you can begin with either left or right. I recommend starting with your dominant hand so that it will be easier to feel comfortable. In addition, your weaker hand will be able to learn from your stronger hand.

The Outside Mallet

Begin with your hand at your side in a relaxed state. Bring your arm up at the elbow and position your hand straight out in front of you with your palm down. Your fingers should be straight with no gaps between them. Your thumb should be against the hand with the thumbnail pointing inward.

Next, take the mallet and place it in between your middle and ring fingers. It should be roughly half-way up the shaft of the mallet and be directly against the webbing of your fingers.

While holding the mallet with your other hand, rotate your hand to a vertical position. The mallet head should be on the outside with your thumbnail facing up.

Next, close your hand while keeping the same vertical position with your thumb facing up. Your pinky and ring fingers should wrap around the mallet and touch the inside of your hand. You shouldn't need to squeeze the mallet to keep it in place. It should angle out and up from your back fingers and the shaft should rest just behind the first knuckle on your middle finger.

Keeping your hand position the same and without adding tension, push the mallet from the base outward. There should be roughly half an inch of the mallet shaft coming out of the back of your hand.

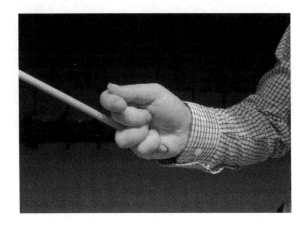

The Inside Mallet

In the same manner as the outside mallet, begin with your arm at your side. Your fingers should be relaxed. Bring your arm up at the elbow and position your hand with your palm facing upward.

Holding the mallet with your free hand, place the end of the mallet at the base of the muscle of your thumb. The mallet shaft should be perpendicular to your hand.

Holding the mallet, rotate your hand inward so the the mallet is now parallel to the floor. Your right hand will rotate counter clockwise with the left rotating clockwise.

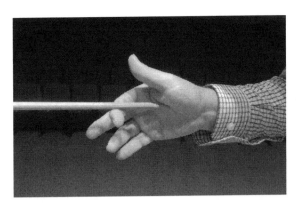

Next, keeping your thumb straight, curve your index finger to where it is pointing inward. With the base of the mallet at your thumb, rest it in the second joint of your index finger. This will create a cantilever and provide stability for the mallet. It is important that your index finger has a natural curve and is pointing in rather than over extending the curve into a closed fist position.

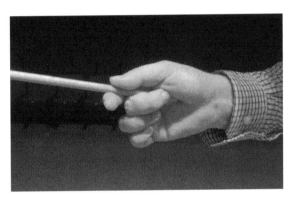

Place your thumb on top of the mallet. It should lay flat with the thumbnail pointing up and crossing the curved index finger. Your middle finger will curve into the hand and rest on the side of the mallet at the base of the thumb. The purpose is to help stabilize the mallet and provide support during interval changes. This is the position of the inside mallet.

Holding Both Mallets Together

Now that we have discussed how to hold both the inside and outside mallets separately, it's time to put them together. I suggest starting with the outside mallet as it is more stationary. When you have the outer mallet securely in place, put the inside mallet in place following the previous instructions. Due to the fact that you will be holding the inside mallet, you will not be able to have your hand completely open. It should be firm but not overly tense. Both inner and outer mallets are supported by the position of the fingers, not be squeezing.

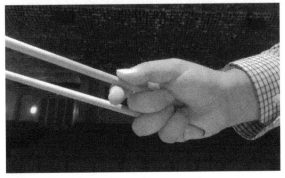

Potential Problems

If the mallets are in the correct position, the mallet heads should be level with each other. The upward angle of the outside mallet will put it level with the inside. If the inner mallet is well above the outer, the base of the mallet is too far back in your hand. Simply pull the mallet out until it falls in line with the outer mallet. Conversely, if the inside mallet is falling below the outer, it is positioned too far out of your hand. Simply push the mallet back into the base of the thumb until is positions itself level with the outer mallet. If the outer mallet is drooping, then the likely cause is that the ring and pinky fingers are not firm enough. Without squeezing, firm the fingers up and try to touch the inside of the palm with the fingers. This should move the outside mallet into place with the inside.

Interval Changes

Now that we have an understanding of how to hold the mallets, we can begin to talk about how they move. Intervals, in addition to the distance between pitches, simply refer to the distance between the heads of the mallets. The ability to change the interval swiftly and smoothly is one of the most important skills that you can have.

Interval changes are done with the inside mallet. The outside mallets remain stationary while the inside mallet moves towards and away from it. I'll break down the interval change into two categories. The first will cover the smaller intervals, i.e. seconds through the sixths. The second will cover larger intervals, including the seventh, octave and beyond. It should be noted that these numbers are subjective. No two sets of hands are identical so the idea of large and small interval positions can vary from person to person. For some, the interval of a fifth may be stretching the limits of the smaller interval technique while some may find that a seventh is still comfortable.

It's also important to know that bar width will affect this. Different brands of instruments will have different widths of bars. Graduated bars will get wider as the notes get lower and can get up to as much as 3.5" in width.

Small Intervals

Your index finger and thumb will move from side to side while the outside mallet remains stationary. The butt end of the inside mallet will move away from the base of your thumb and towards the middle of your hand.

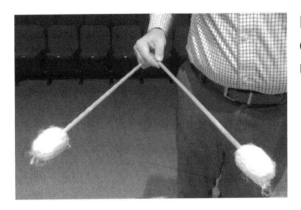

In addition, the movement of of your thumb and index finger will cause the inside mallet to roll as it moves toward and away from the outside mallet.

One of the most common habits is for this finger to wrap around the mallet making a fist rather than a relaxed curve. This problem is twofold: First, it creates unnecessary tension in the hand and second, it inhibits the fluid side to side movement needed to adjust the interval.

Large Intervals

The larger intervals require the inside mallet to move to a new position in your hand. This technique is often called "locking the octave" due to the fact the inside mallet feels as though it's locked into place. It creates stability within the technique while keeping the outside mallet in the same position in your hand. While the inside mallet can still move, it does limit the range of motion of that mallet.

The base of the mallet travels in an arch from your thumb to the base of the middle finger in one smooth motion. As this is happening, your middle finger extends out from the palm of your hand into a natural curve.

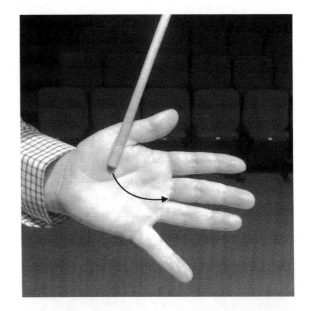

With the end resting underneath the base of the middle finger, place the mallet on the side of the second joint of that same finger. Make sure that you extend the finger enough to give the mallet enough support. If it's not extended enough, you'll lose leverage and the grip will feel unstable.

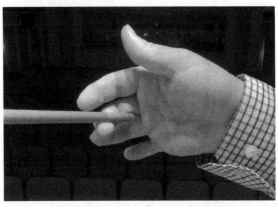

Extend your index finger around the front of the mallet and place your thumb on top. There should be a natural curve with the index finger that follows the curve of the middle finger.

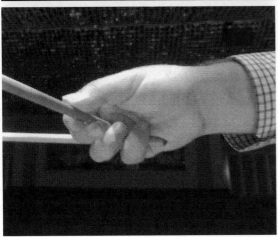

The ring and pinky fingers should stay in their original position, and you should have a similar range of motion with your wrist. There is no need to squeeze the mallets to keep them in your hand.

There are two problems that may show up. First, avoid clinching your thumb over the top of the mallet. This will create unnecessary tension in your hand and severely cripple the ability to adjust the interval once it's in position.

Secondly, avoid "reaching" with the outside mallet. Your pinky and ring finger should remain as they are in the smaller interval technique, that is to say, wrapped around the mallet with the fingertips touching the inside of the hand. Avoid opening up your hand to put the responsibility of the interval change on the outside mallet. Remember, the inside mallet is responsible for interval changes, not the outside.

Review

- Keep your hands vertical. Resist the urge to turn your hands horizontal.

- Your pinky and ring fingers wrap around the outside mallet with the fingertips touching the inside of the hand. Your fingers should be firm without squeezing.

- Your thumb should rest on top of the mallet over the second joint of the index finger.

- Your index fingers should be pointed inward towards each other.

- Avoid clenching the index finger to make a fist.

- Make sure your wrist is in a straight alignment with the arm. There should be no unnatural bends or angles at your wrist.

- The interval changes are the responsibility of the inside mallet. The outside mallet remains stationary while the inside mallet moves toward and away from it.

- Regardless of the size of the interval, keep your fingers in place without squeezing.

2
Doubles

The first stroke that we will be talking about is the double vertical stroke. It is perhaps the most basic of the stroke types and will become the foundation for many of the strokes discussed later. It is, like the name suggests, both mallets moving together to play two notes simultaneously. Keep in mind that the motion for the stroke comes from the wrist. The fingers' primary function of the grip is for holding the mallets and for interval changes.

Begin by simply laying that mallets on the bars at a comfortable interval, such as a fifth. If you need to, take a moment to make sure that the mallets haven't shifted in your hand and that it is still in the correct vertical position. Next, gently push the mallet heads into the bars with the wrist. This should cause your wrist to slightly pop upward. Pull the mallet heads back using your wrist. Try to avoid having the mallets travel up. Try to visualize strings tied to the mallets heads and that there is someone behind you pulling the strings so that the mallets travel back toward you. This will create a dip at the base of your forearm and hand. Finally, throw the mallet heads into the bars and return to the same position. Make sure that the wrist remains flexible through the stroke. Avoid locking your wrist into position and using the forearm to deliver the stroke. Also make sure that you don't stop the stroke at the bottom only to have to restart the motion upward.

Start with one hand, preferably your dominant hand. As with learning how to hold the mallets, let your dominant hand help the weaker hand. Also, a few text books or pillows will do as much good as a $14,000 5.0 octave marimba. Begin with one stroke and evaluate. Make sure that the mallets have not shifted in your hand and repeat. As the motion becomes comfortable, move from playing one stroke to two, three, four and so on.

Stationary Exercises

This first exercise uses the double vertical stroke in each hand, first separately then with both hands together. Try to keep your arms from slowing rising higher and higher. Your hands shouldn't be at the same level as the bars, but slightly above. Repeat each measure until you feel comfortable before moving to the next measure. Again, take time in between to make sure that the mallets haven't shifted in your hands.

As the interval gets smaller, avoid turning the hands inward to a horizontal position. Also make sure that your fingers don't clinch to make a fist. Pull the inside mallet toward the outside.

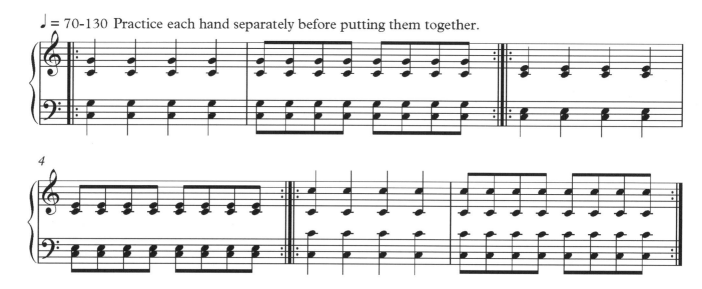

For the larger intervals, make sure that the octave is locked into place and that your thumb has not clinched over the top and your back fingers are not reaching. Even at the largest intervals, you will still be able to use the wrist to initiate the stroke while staying relaxed and keeping the fingers in place.

Shifting

    Shifting refers to the movement from one position to another. This can be done either within an interval change or by the movement of the arm and hand into a new position. The key to shifting is to do it as efficiently as possible and the best way is to combine horizontal and vertical motions. This combined motion forms an arc when the rebound of the stroke travels with the horizontal motion to the next position.

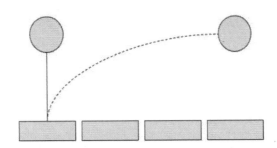

Example 1 shows the arc formed by the combined motions.

Example 2 shows the rebound of the mallet moving upward before moving horizontally over to the new position.

Example 3 shows the mallet traveling down to strike the bar. It stays close to the bar, moves horizontally to the new location and moves upward to prepare for the next stroke.

Combining Double Vertical Strokes and Shifting

    Now that we have talked about how to properly shift, we can apply it to the marimba. At first, make sure that you are shifting efficiently. Look for the arc created by the combination of horizontal and vertical motions. If needed, shift slowly to make sure you have an arc. Aim to be in position in time **before** the rest, not in the middle of it. The shift should feel identical with or without rests.

R.H. followed by L.H. 8vb

This exercise develops shifting from the large interval to the smaller one. Practice the interval change alone before playing the exercises. It should feel like you're throwing the mallet from one position in the hand to another. Remember, shift **before** the next beat.

R.H. followed by L.H. 8vb

Now let's work on finding your limits between the small and large intervals. It can be easier when there is a larger distance due to the energy required. Whether its a fifth, sixth or seventh, find where your limit is and practice just those intervals. Once it's comfortable, play each exercise and apply what you've practiced when you need to switch.

Now that there is familiarity with shifting within the interval change, we can introduce the arms and body. These exercises will use chords in root position and inversions to get your arms moving from side to side. Remember, the arms move, the wrists play the strokes, and the fingers hold the mallets and change the intervals. As the exercise becomes more and more comfortable, you can start removing rests.

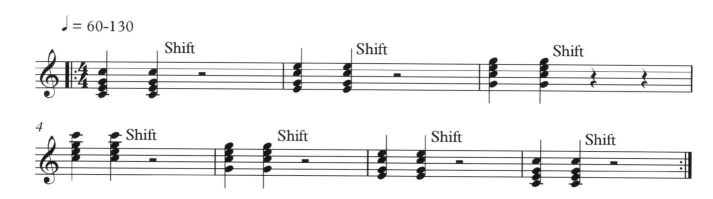

Shifting Between Manuals

By adding backward and forward motions, shifting between the upper and lower manuals will bring new challenges. You'll want to maintain a comfortable playing position. When you have the outside mallet on the upper manual and the inside mallet on the lower manual, turn the hands inward to a more flat or horizontal position. In addition, the elbow will need to move away from the body to keep the proper alignment of the forearm and wrist.

Avoid bending the wrist inward to reach the intervals. This will take away the leverage that you'll need to play the stroke. It's also really uncomfortable.

If the inside mallet falls on the upper manual with the outside on the lower, pull your wrist into your torso. This will create an inward angle with the hand and forearm. It will move away from a more traditional up and down motion to more of a rotation with the forearm. In either case, as the intervals get smaller, the rotation or angle of the wrist will become more pronounced.

This exercise works on shifting back and forth between manuals. In addition to correct shifting technique, the elbow plays a key role. Moving the elbow in and out of the body will allow the forearm and wrist to maintain the correct alignment.

Here we'll explore different keys. The first inversion of each usually provides the most difficulty. You will either have both outside or both inside mallets on the upper manuals. Remove the rests as you get more comfortable.

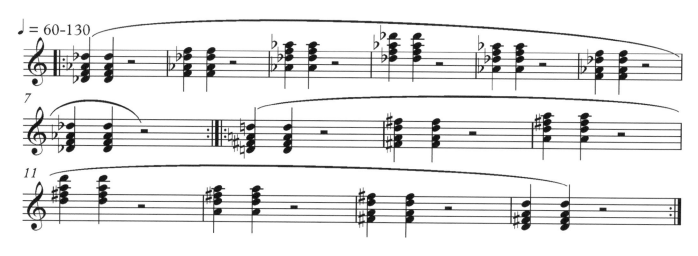

Review

- Initiate the Double Vertical stroke from the wrist. Put the mallets on the bars, slightly push the heads into the bars and pull the mallets back. Avoid lifting the mallets up.

- Throw the mallets into the bars. Avoid locking the wrist and using your arm for the stroke.

- Don't stop in the middle of the stroke. Make it one continuous motion.

- Interval changes come from the inside mallets. The outside mallets remain stationary.

- When shifting, either as an interval change or moving the arms, combine the horizontal and vertical motions. Avoid, stopping the mallet in the middle of the shift.

- Shift early and quickly.

- When the outside mallet is on the upper manual, turn the hand inward to flatten the hand. When the inside mallet is on the upper manual, pull the wrist inward towards the body.

3

Singles

The next stroke that we will discuss is the single independent stroke. Like the name suggests, it involves playing with one of the mallets while the other remains unused. Like the double vertical stroke, both mallets will start at the same height. There are a variety of uses for the this stroke which include playing the melodic line of an accompanied part or playing passages that only need two mallets.

The Outside Mallet

The goal is to be able to use one of the mallets without the other moving along with it. Since the unused mallet is also in your hand, expecting to have absolutely no movement is unrealistic. The motion that we are wanting to avoid is an excessive up and down motion that follows the mallet that's being used. The unused mallet will rotate along with the hand and it also may dip slightly. Begin in the same position that you would use for a double vertical stroke. Remember to use the wrist rather than the arm. The single independent motion is a combination of the downward motion of the double vertical stroke with an outward rotation of the hand. It should feel like the hand is rotating around the point where the inside mallet is in your hand. This will create a rotation in the mallet head without letting it move up and down with the other mallet.

In order to get comfortable with the motion, do it slowly. As you begin to feel more confident, start to speed it up. The motion is the same regardless of speed. Once again, a textbook and mirror will do wonders. There are two potential problems that can show up. First, if you see the inside mallet traveling down with the outside mallet, there is too much downward motion in the stroke. Compensate for this by increasing the amount of rotation with your hand. Second, if the inside mallet moves up and over the hand it means that there is too much rotation of the hand. Increase the amount of downward motion in your hand to compensate.

The Inside Mallet

The inside mallet also uses a combination of downward motion and a rotation. The rotation, however, is inward. Once again, begin in the same position as you would before a double vertical stroke. Perhaps the best way to describe it is to rotate the hand towards the thumb. The thumb should feel like it is leading the way with the back of the hand popping upward. As with practicing the outside mallet, begin the motion slowly. The motion at the slow speed will be identical at a fast speed. Additionally, gently holding the unused mallet in place will also help the hand adjust to the motion.

Again, two issues may show up. If you see the outside mallet dipping down while you are playing, there is too much downward motion and not enough rotation. If you see the outside mallet popping up and over the hand, there is too much rotation and not enough downward motion.

With both inside and outside mallets, make sure that you're not locking up the wrist and using your forearm to deliver the stroke.

Exercises

This first exercise will begin to develop the motion of the single independent stroke. Start with the longer note values. This will allow you to be able to think about what you're doing without having to play anything too complex. It should feel the same at all tempos and note values. This exercise should be played with all four mallets individually. Take the repeats until you become comfortable with the different note values then, pull the repeats and play it as one phrase.

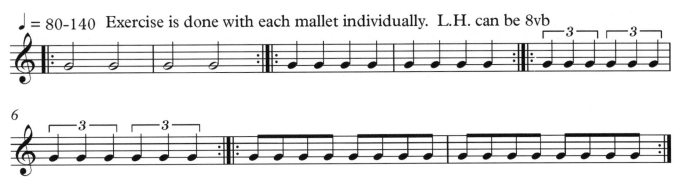

For this exercise, keep the mallets over the correct notes when you aren't playing them. It may help to start at a softer dynamic level and work your way to a louder one. Once the interval of the perfect fifth feels comfortable, expand to other intervals. Thirds and octaves will feel different from one another so keeping the motion consistent between them is important.

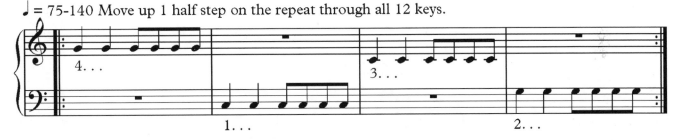

Now we'll introduce shifting. Remember to keep the smooth motion of the single independent stroke consistent. As discussed in chapter 2, the shift should be a combination of horizontal and vertical movement. In this case, the vertical movement is produced by the single independent upstroke with the horizontal movement coming from the side to side and back and forth motion of the arms. Practice this exercises using each mallet individually as well as alternating between mallets 2 and 3.

This exercise will help develop the single independent stroke within running scale patterns. Once again, let the muscle groups be responsible for their part. Wrists take care of the single independent stroke with the arms taking care of the lateral, forward and backward movement. With each of these exercises, explore other keys to continually test yourself. Don't play everything in C major.

For the final exercise, let your arms guide the hands into place. Avoid lifting them up with each stroke. They should move smoothly from side to side while your wrists and hands play the single independent strokes. Try "following the line". This means that you'll get louder as the notes get higher and softer as they get lower. Again, playing the exercise in different keys will present new challenges.

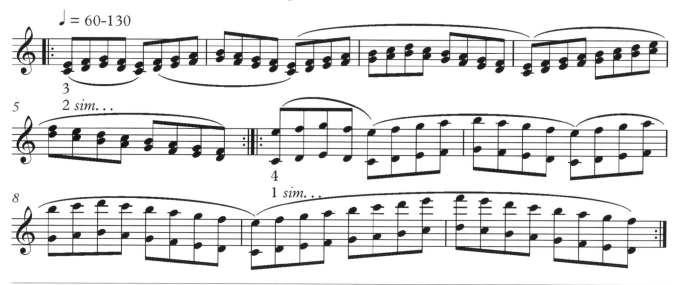

Review

- The single independent stroke begins in the same way as the double vertical stroke. Both mallets should be at the same height.

- The motion is a combination of a downward motion with a rotation of the wrist. Outward towards in the direction of the first joint of the index finger for the outside mallet.

- The inward motion goes in the direction of the thumb for the inside mallet.

- For the outside mallet stroke; if the inside mallet dips then there is too much downward motion and not enough rotation. If the inside mallet comes up and over, there is too much rotation and not enough downward motion.

- For the inside mallet stroke; if the outside mallet dips then there is too much downward motion and not enough rotation. If the outside mallet moves up and over toward the inside, there is too much rotation and not enough downward motion.

- When shifting, the wrist is responsible for the stroke and the arm is responsible for the lateral, forward and backwards movement. Avoid mixing those responsibilities.

4

Singles Part 2

The single alternating stroke is an extension of the single independent stroke that will constantly alternate between mallets. Like the previous two strokes, we will start with both mallets up and level with each other.   What makes it unique is that it will have a speed limit. If the tempo is too slow it will then become a series of single independent strokes that alternate between mallets. If the tempo moves too fast, the muscles won't be able to keep up and will be forced to switch from a bouncing motion to a pure rotation of the arm. Since there are no two sets of hands that are the same, this speed limit varies from person to person. It's important to find your speed limits.

Begin with the mallets at the same horizontal level, keeping the forearm down and the hand pulled back at the wrist. The motion for this stroke is similar to a bouncing motion. What you want to avoid is for the arm to produce a pure rotation motion. This will cause the mallets to come into the bars at an angle rather than straight down, thus causing the sound quality to reduce dramatically. Additionally, you will have to stop and restart the motion for each stroke. This bouncing motion is a natural extension of the motion of the single independent stroke that keeps your hands in constant motion. The outside mallet rotates towards the first knuckle of the index finger before bouncing back into position. The inside mallet rotates towards the thumb and then bounces back into position.

Exercises

Remember to begin and end with both mallets in the same position. Like the earlier strokes, begin with the dominant hand and let the weaker hand learn by its example. Practice these exercises with the left hand down an octave.

Start at the slower marked tempo and work your way up from there. Again, the speed limit varies from person to person so this is not a set tempo, rather a suggestion. As you are speeding up, remember to keep the motion the same. Faster tempos don't mean changing the motion or adding tension. It simply means that you need to move your hands faster. As it becomes more comfortable, experiment with smaller and larger intervals such as the second, octave, and everything in between.

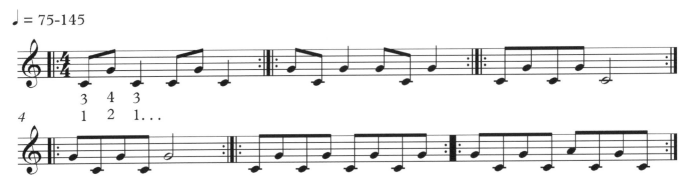

Now that we have an understanding of how the single alternating stroke works, the next step is will be to add interval changes and shifts. The objective, as in all of the previous shifting exercises, is to complete the shift well before you need to play. You should aim to be over the new bar and ready to initiate the stroke as opposed to still moving horizontally when you need to be moving down. Once again, start with the dominant hand before moving to the weaker hand. Keep practicing with your hands separate and with the left hand down the octave.

For the next exercises, bring out the rising and falling lines while keeping the the repeated note the same. Try following the line so that the dynamics rise and fall along with the notes. If you're working on a piece of music and you're not quite sure how to shape the phrase, following the line can be a great place to start and branch out from.

The next step is to put the hands together. Keep in mind that the motion doesn't change and that the difficulty comes from coordinating your hands. If the parallel motion of the first measure proves to be awkward, try the second measure. In many cases playing the outside and inside mallets together at first is easier.

Once you have a greater amount of comfort putting the hands together, move towards the next exercise. Start with your hands separate followed by putting them together. Remember to shift early.

The final exercise deals with single alternating strokes that are offset from each other. This is a very common figure found in the solo marimba repertoire. It's important to keep in mind that while they are offset, the stroke is still the same. Strive to keep the motion consistent between the parallel figures and the offset ones.

Review

- The single alternating stroke uses a rocking back and forth motion that is a natural extension of the single independent stroke.
- Avoid using a pure rotation of the arm. This will cause the mallet to come in at an angle rather than straight into the bar.
- Additionally, you'll have to constantly stop and restart each stroke.

- There is a speed limit. If you go too slow it will be a single independent stroke. If you go too fast it will become an independent roll.
- This speed limit is different for everyone. Know your muscles and how fast they can go.
- Shifts and interval changes are the same. Know the responsibilities of the fingers, wrist and arms.

5

Doubles Part 2

The next stroke that we'll talk about is the double lateral stroke. It can be best compared to a double stroke on a snare drum, that is to say that one motion will produce two notes. While it begins in the same position as the techniques that have been discussed, the actual motion is very different. Like the single independent stroke, there are two different motions depending on which mallet you start with.

Inside-Out

The double lateral stroke, regardless of which mallet you are starting with, will begin in the same level position as each of the other strokes. In order to learn it, we'll break it up into separate motions. Begin with the inside mallet on the bar with the outside still in position above the bar. It should look similar to the single independent stroke.

Next rotate the wrist inward. It should be a very quick motion, similar to a flick of the wrist, that will cause the inside mallet to pop up as the outside mallet plays the stroke. Finally, the outside mallet should rebound back to the same level as the inside mallet and into the standard position.

The motion should be a rolling motion at the wrist. As the rotation becomes more natural, add the first stroke and combine the two movements in to one continuous motion. Remember to begin and end in the same position. Avoid lowering and raising the forearm to augment the stroke. Think down and up with the wrist.

Outside-In

Start with the outside mallet on the bar. The inside mallet should still be elevated with the other mallet on the bar. Next, roll the hand outward in a quick motion. Think about a flick of the wrist. This rotation will produce the note with the inside mallet and cause the outside mallet to pop up. Finally, continue the motion with the inside mallet following the outside back into its original position. As the motion becomes more comfortable, add the outside stroke to make one, continuous motion that will produce both notes.

Exercises

This first exercise will help combine the motions required to play the double lateral stroke. While the stroke is one motion, the first movement is in essence a single independent stroke. Remember that the mallets will start at the same level. Focus on the down beats in all four measures especially when the second note is introduced. For the double lateral strokes, strive for one smooth motion. Avoid stopping and restarting half way through.

For the next exercise, focus on maintaining the feel of the eighth note patterns when transitioning to the sixteenth notes. This should help you feel the larger, single motion. Try to think of it in the same way as a double stroke roll. Often times the best way to practice is to take the roll out and work on the underlying rhythm. It's the same concept here. It should not only help you develop a strong sense of rhythmic clarity but to keep a steady tempo as well. Try to feel the eighth and quarter notes in the second example, rather than each individual sixteenth note. Also, experiment with larger and smaller intervals.

Next, we'll add shifting and some small interval changes. Remember to be in place and ready to play as early as possible. As you become more comfortable, take the rests out and connect the arpeggios. When you have arpeggios that use both manuals, the arms should use a pushing and pulling motion. The motion of the wrist remains the same while the arms will be pushing up to the upper manual or pulling the hand back towards the lower.

This final exercise will introduce new variations of double lateral strokes. Try to feel the larger note groups, i.e. the quarter note, as opposed to all of the smaller notes. If needed, put a gentle accent on each downbeat. This will give the sixtuplet a much smoother sound as opposed to each of the six notes sounding exactly the same.

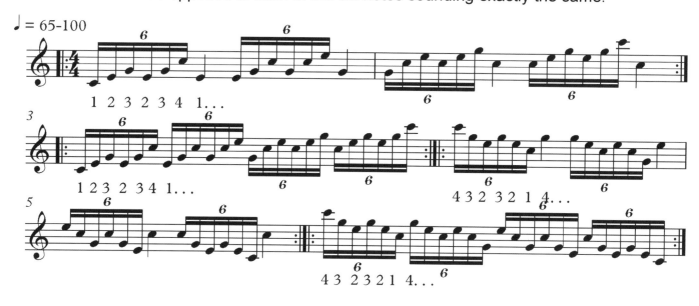

Review

- The double lateral stroke is akin to the double stroke. It is one motion that will produce two notes.

- The motion features a rotation of your hand. The mallets should start and end at the same horizontal level. Keep your arms down and your hand pulled back at the wrist.

- When the outside mallet is played first, your hand will rotate outward before returning to the original position.

- When the inside mallet is played first, your hand will rotate inward before returning to the original position.

- Try to feel the larger note values, such as eighth and quarter notes, rather than each individual note within the stroke.

6

The Roll

The final topic that we'll discuss doesn't deal with a specific technique or stroke type. Instead, we will be talking about the different types of rolls that are used on the marimba. There are three in all: the traditional hand to hand roll, the Musser or "ripple" roll, and the independent or "one-handed" roll. The purpose of the roll is to simulate a sustained note. The natural sustain of each bar can vary from instrument to instrument and even from room to room so it's important to be comfortable with a variety of different roll speeds to be able to imitate this sustain in any environment.

The Traditional Roll

The traditional or hand to hand roll is the extension of the two mallet rolling technique into four mallets. In this case, both mallets in each hand will be played at the same time. Basically, it's the alternation of double vertical strokes between the hands. Avoid locking your wrists and using your arms to play the roll strokes. A fluid and relaxed motion with the wrists will make the roll look and sound like a sustained note.

This first exercise will help develop the traditional roll. It's simply a succession of major chords that rise chromatically. The goal is to move smoothly through the exercise without any interruptions or sudden changes in roll speed. Try starting the roll and leading with the left hand. The notes in the lower range tend to get to the audience a little slower than those in the upper. By starting and leading with the left hand, the audience will hear smooth transitions rather than the higher notes followed by the lower. This can be awkward at first, but getting into the habit early will help your rolls move more smoothly. When you're shifting up to the next chord, don't change what your hands are playing. The arms will take the majority of the responsibility of the shift while the hands continue to roll.

Let's take a look at a chorale by Johann Sebastian Bach. Even though it isn't notated, we are going to roll all of the notes. A great way to practice, not only chorales but any extended roll passage, is to take the rolls out and replace them with block chords. You will pick a note value that works will all of the rhythms in the chorale. Sixteenth note triplets or thirty second notes work well in this case. This will give you a chance to learn the piece while maintaining a steady tempo. In addition it will help you learn the shifts and how to do them quickly and efficiently. Once you can play through the chorale this way, switch to traditional rolls.

Since this was not written with the marimba in mind, there might be some wide intervals. If you have trouble reaching some of the lower notes, simply bring them up the octave to make it a little more manageable. Since we want to imitate a long tone, use a soft mallet for these chorales. Avoid locking up the wrists and using your arms to play the rolls. Their responsibility is to move the hands into position.

Wer nur den lieben Gott Läßt walten

J.S. Bach

Musser or "Ripple" Rolls

The Musser or "ripple" roll uses double lateral strokes in place of double vertical strokes. This will result in each individual note of a chord sounding rather than two at a time. The order of the roll strokes is 1-2-4-3. Starting with the left hand achieves the same balance as with the traditional roll. Using 4-3 in the right hand will also help that balance. If the highest note is always the last note heard, it will automatically draw the listener's ear toward it.

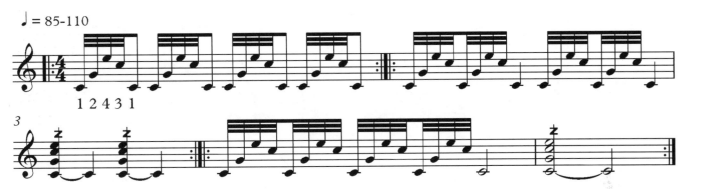

The Musser roll is not metered, that is to say it does not have a set number of strokes within the note value. However, it is beneficial to work on them in this way. The purpose is to develop the speed that is needed to create the roll while helping with dynamic and rhythmic consistency. Try playing the exercise at the top of pg. 33 with Musser rolls in place of traditional rolls.

Independent Rolls

The one handed or independent roll allows you to play a roll with one hand while the other remains independent, hence the name. In chapter 4, we talked about the speed limits of the single alternating stroke. If you go too fast the the motion changes from a bounce to a pure rotation. This rotation is what makes the roll. It is perhaps the most unique of all of the strokes due to the fact that it does not use the normal motion of the wrist. The hand, wrist, and forearm all take part in this rotation and it causes a rapid alternation of the mallets.

The goal of these first exercises is to develop rhythmic consistency within the roll. As with the musser rolls, it is not metered. However, getting in the habit of hearing and feeling rhythmic consistency in the roll will help with making it smooth. Make sure that you switch from a single independent stroke with the eighth notes to a pure rotation for the sixteenth notes. Rhythm and dynamics stay consistent through the rotations. Avoid simply rotating your arm as fast as possible without regards to controlling speed and dynamics.

As the exercise become more comfortable, add four sixteenth notes on to each group. Continue to add them in groups of four as you get more comfortable. Once again, strive for rhythmic and dynamic consistency in the roll. As this interval becomes comfortable, explore larger and smaller intervals. An independent roll at the octave feels much different than a roll at the third.

Endurance is another difficult part of independent rolls. It requires a lot of energy to keep the rolls going, and fatigue can set it as the they get longer. For the next exercise you will repeat each measure four times before moving to the next. After you get through all six repeated measures, repeat the entire process. Instead of repeating each measure four times, play each six times, followed by eight and ten times each. As the fatigue sets in focus on keeping the rhythm and dynamic level between the mallets constant. If you get tired, reduce the dynamic level and try to relax. Try to avoid adding tension and "muscling" it out. Over time you will develop endurance, and it's extremely important to create good habits. If you build a habit of tensing up when ever you feel fatigued, you will run into problems during a crucial time in a performance.

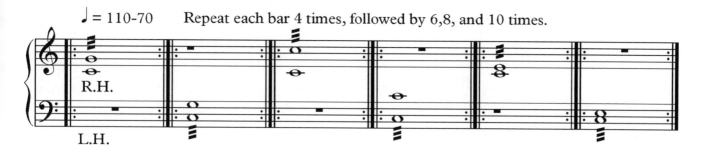

♩ = 110-70   Repeat each bar 4 times, followed by 6,8, and 10 times.

Perhaps the most unique aspect of the independent roll is the fact that it allows you to play a longer melodic line while the other hand accompanies it. In order to be able to play these lines independent of the roll, play the previous exercise and start off by playing something simple, such as double vertical quarter notes, with the free hand. As you become more comfortable, expand to other rhythms including eighths, sixteenths, and triplets as well as the different stroke types that we have talked about. Finally, improvise in and out of time to work on developing true independence of the hands.

Review

- Rolls are meant to mimic long tones. Smooth motions regardless of the type of roll are crucial.

- Leading with the left hand will help provide a more even beginning to the roll and will also produce a smoother sounding line.

- With traditional rolls, remember to use your wrists. Locking up and pumping your arms will not only lead to fatigue, but it will also produce a roll that sounds more like a succession of notes rather than one long tone.

- The Musser roll isn't metered, but the rhythms and dynamics between mallets needs to be consistent.

- Just like the Musser roll, the independent roll needs consistency.

- Be able to control the dynamic level and the space between roll strokes.

- Avoid simply rotating your arm as fast as possible without regards to dynamic or rhythmic consistency.

- When fatigue sets in, lower the volume and relax. Don't tense up and "muscle" through it. You will build strength in the correct way.

Before we get to the music

A little bit about mallets. . .

- *Rattan or Birch*
  - Rattan is less rigid and it will flex and bend while you play. It may also have a larger diameter than birch.
  - Birch will use a thinner diameter (5/16") and it will be more rigid and lighter than rattan.
- *Mallet Shape*
  - Round mallet heads will be more "single toned".
  - The sound will stay consistent as the angle of the mallet changes.
  - With the more oval or oblong shape, you have more timbre or color options depending on the angle of the mallet.
- *Mallet Core*
  - Plastic cores will have a brighter tone. Having a bright sound means the higher overtones are more prevalent.
  - Rubber cores will have a darker tone. This means that the lower overtones will be brought out.
- *Single tone v. Multi-tone*
  - Single tone mallets use a consistent wrapping. The timbre or color of the mallet stays consistent at all dynamic levels.
  - Multi-tone mallets have a tighter wrapping on the interior and a more loose level on the outside. The sound will become brighter as the volume increases.

A little bit about practice. . .

(not the game, just practice)

- *Slow practice is good practice.*
  - Give yourself a chance to have a little success right away. Slow practice will let you get the music in your mind while teaching your muscles the correct movements in a relaxed state.
  - Starting off with a tempo that is too fast may lead to mental mistakes while making the piece feel more difficult than it really is.
- *The metronome is great, until it isn't. . .*
  - Use the metronome as a learning tool but don't become dependent on it. As you get comfortable with what you're doing, decrease the amount that you're using it.
  - Find different ways to use it, such as every other beat or once per measure.
  - Don't let it become a crutch that holds you together.
- *Practice what's difficult about the music away from the music.*
  - If you see a difficult passage that uses a technique that you aren't comfortable with, find or make up an exercise to fix it before you get to that part of the piece.
  - Be honest with yourself about what you can't do and be proactive about fixing it.
- *Seriously, slow practice is good practice.*
  - Slow practice will work wonders on the first day of learning a new piece all the way to the day of the performance.

7
Music: Volume I

Drew Worden *Babo*

Aaron Staebell *Bountiful*

Michael Burritt *Eastern Promises*

Matthew Curlee *Nocturne*

Elliot Cole *Evensong*

Drew Worden

Babo

Drew Worden (b. 1988) is an arts organizer, drummer, percussionist, and composer. Drew currently lives in Boston where he is the Program Manager of Entrepreneurial Musicianship at the New England Conservatory. Prior to his appointment at NEC, Drew earned the Master of Music degree and Arts Leadership Certificate from the Eastman School of Music. While at Eastman, Drew was a post-graduate fellow in Musicians' Health, where he and a team of healthcare providers developed wellness practices for performing artists.

Drew has served as session producer for recording projects at the University of Notre Dame and Eastman School of Music with Third Coast Percussion and Michael Burritt, traveled to Ireland as a drumset artist for the 2015 Recording Festival with his rock band Stegall, presented workshops and masterclasses on Musicians' Health, and launched an online store for his self-published compositions. As a classical contemporary percussionist, he has performed at the Darmstadt Internationales Musikinstitut in Germany, and studied at the So Percussion Summer Institute at Princeton University.

As a composer, Drew has written original soundtracks for the documentary Spiritus (finalist, Student Academy Awards) and the children's book series Yum & Yuk. His works for percussion are performed frequently at conservatories and universities with recent performances in France, Colombia, Germany, and across the US. Andrew performs regularly with his duo Dr. Ax, the rock band Stegall, the multidisciplinary ensemble Sticks, Strings, and Paint, and the East Side Brass Band. He is also a co-founder of The Healthy Musician Project. His music is self-published online, with select compositions available from Malletech and Steve Weiss Music.

Learn more at: www.drewworden.com and www.TheHealthyMusicianProject.com

- *Balance*
  - Know where the melodic line is and help your listener hear it.
  - In the A section, it's in the top or soprano voice
  - In the B section, it switches to the bottom or bass.
  - Have the hand that has the melody play slightly louder than the other.
- *Correct technique*
  - *Babo* uses mostly double vertical strokes.
  - Remember that the wrist is responsible for the strokes and the arms will take care of the shifts.
  - Don't let the arm do the job of the wrist.
- *Keep comfortable hand positions*
  - When you have to play an accidental with the outside mallet, turn the hand to a more flat position.
  - When the accidental is with the inside mallet, pull the wrist to your body and create an angle with the hand and arm.
  - This will keep the wrist and forearm in a better alignment rather than having an uncomfortable outward bend at the wrist.
  - The degree of how much you need to rotate the hand or pull the wrist in depends on the interval.
  - A smaller interval means a more pronounced movement.
- *Think big*
  - Try to think of the repeated chords in the middle section as one long note instead of four individual ones.
  - Connect the measures to make long phrases.
  - Connect the phrases to give the larger section musical context.
  - Make the individual notes, measures, phrases and sections work together to say something meaningful.

Mallets Used: Malletech - CN9, 3-CN14

.3 marimba

for Josh, Jenni, and Oliver

babo

commissioned by Mark Boseman

Drew Worden
2016

Più mosso
Lyrically

2

41

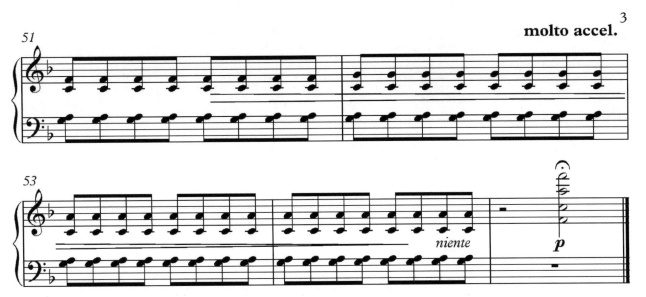

niente

p

Columbia, MO
May, 2016

Supplemental Exercises I

These exercises are inspired by Drew Worden's *Babo*. Aim for a range in tempo of 90 to 140 for the quarter note.

Continue through the scale and in all 12 keys.

Aaron Staebell
Bountiful

Aaron Staebell is a drummer, composer and educator who hails from Orchard Park, NY and has lived in Rochester, NY for the last 15 years. Jazz legend Bob Brookmeyer described Aaron as having "swing, energy and musicianship to a remarkable degree" and said, "I would hire him. My utmost praise." Having earned both undergraduate and graduate degrees from the Eastman School of Music, Staebell is an in-demand both locally and nationwide.

Aaron's debut album, Bending and Breaking was released in July of 2011. The album consists of 8 original compositions that span a wide variety of styles and moods. The album was immediately chosen for the "New and Noteworthy" category on iTunes jazz and has gone on to receive much critical acclaim. Allaboutjazz.com called it "…a debut filled with energy, enthusiasm and invention…" while the Toronto Star referred to Staebell as "…energized and eclectic and a weirdo you don't want to miss."

He is also active as an educator, as the director of bands at Greece Olympia High School as well as freelance private lessons. He is a champion of innovation and new perspectives in music education. His jazz ensemble at Greece Odyssey Academy was known around the region for its commitment to performing new, modern works for jazz ensemble. In his time there, the band played world premieres by Fred Sturm, Tom Davis and Staebell himself, earning them annual performances at the Rochester International Jazz Festival.

In addition to Rich Thompson, Staebell's teachers have included John Hollenbeck, John Riley, Tom Davis and Bill Dobbins. He has played with Tony Malaby, Maria Schneider, Ryan Truesdell, Gap Mangione and others.

He lives with his wife Sarah, who is also a music educator, and his daughter, Keeley. More about Staebell can be found at www.aaronstaebell.com.

- **Correct Technique**
  - *Bountiful* makes excellent use of the double vertical stroke.
  - Remember to initiate the stroke from the wrist.
  - Avoid locking up the wrist to us the forearm or opening and closing the fingers to "whip" the mallets into the bars.
  - When the outside mallet is on the upper manual and the inside is on the lower, flatten the hand and extend the elbow out.
  - Avoid extreme outward bends and angles at the wrist.
- **Explore the space**
  - This piece uses a great deal of space by way of rests and fermatas.
  - As percussionists, it can be uncomfortable due to our comfort in busy rhythms.
  - Try not to hurry through the rests. Also, make sure that every fermata isn't the same length.
  - If every break is identical, the listener will pick up on it and it will become predictable.
- **Don't change the motion**
  - As the block chord eighth notes turn into offset sixteenth notes, avoid changing the motion in your hands.
  - The movements are identical.
  - The only thing that changes is the rhythm.
- **Explore the characters**
  - There are a number of different characters and themes in this piece.
  - Through phrasing, tempo and attitude, give each of them their own unique style.
  - Try to have contrast in feeling from one to the next.
  - Above all else, have fun and strive to be happy.

Mallets Used: Malletech - Overly soft CN9, 2-MB8, MB13

BOUNTIFUL
(4.3 Octave Version)

Aaron Staebell

Composed for Mark Boseman's "A Musical Guide to Four Mallets"

Rainbow Lake, NY
2016

Supplemental Exercises II

These exercises are inspired by Aaron Staebell's *Bountiful*. Aim for a range in tempo of 75 to 115 for the quarter note.

"**Bountiful**" makes extensive use of the double vertical stroke. It is inspired by the majesty of the Adirondack Mountains, where my family lives for part of the year. The word "bountiful" has multiple appropriate definitions. First, it can mean 'abundant' or 'large', which the mountains most certainly are. Secondly, and more importantly, it can mean 'generous'. I love visiting the camp, as it reminds me of how much the world gives to us. This piece is my way of giving thanks to the region that has brought us so much happiness.

Michael Burritt

Eastern Promises

Having performed on four continents and more than forty states Michael Burritt is one of the World's leading percussion soloists. He is in frequent demand performing concert tours and master classes throughout the United States, Europe, Asia, Australia and Canada. Mr. Burritt has been soloist with the Dallas Wind Symphony, Omaha Symphony, Chautauqua Symphony Orchestra, Richmond Symphony Orchestra, Ju Percussion Group (Taiwan), Percussion Art Quartet (Germany), Amores Percussion Group (Spain), Nexus and the Third Coast Percussion. Mr. Burritt has three solo as well as numerous chamber recordings. In 2006 he recorded the Joseph Schwantner Percussion Concerto with the Calgary Wind Ensemble on the Albany label and is soon to release a new recording of solo and chamber works by Alejandro Viñao. Mr. Burritt has just finished a recording project with Nexus his new work Home Trilogy, commissioned by the group.

Mr. Burritt is also an artist/clinician and product design/consultant for Malletech, where he has developed his own line of signature marimba mallets and recently collaborated on the design of the MJB Marimba. He is an artist / educational clinician with the Zildjian Company and Evans Drum Heads. Mr. Burritt was a member of the Percussive Arts Society Board of Directors from 1996 - 2008, is a contributing editor for Percussive Notes Magazine and was chairman of the PAS Keyboard Committee from 2004 – 2010.

Michael Burritt is currently Professor of Percussion and head of the department at The Eastman School of Music where is only the third person in the history of the school to hold this position. Prior to his appointment at Eastman Mr. Burritt was Professor of Percussion at Northwestern University from 1995-2008 where he developed a program of international distinction. Mr. Burritt received his Bachelor and Master of Music Degrees, as well as the prestigious Performers Certificate from the Eastman School of Music in Rochester, New York. More can be found at http://www.michaelburritt.com

- **Mixed stroke types**
  - *Eastern Promises* has a healthy mixture of double vertical and single independent strokes.
  - Make sure that you're comfortable with both motions separately before putting them together.
  - If the combination of motions in the music is awkward, pull them out of the piece and practice them using an exercise or improvisation.
- **Balance**
  - The melody primarily lies in the left hand. Make sure that it isn't covered by the right hand.
  - Because the accompaniment is not only in a higher register but also a series of repeated eight notes, you'll have to work harder for the melody to be heard.
  - Explore even softer dynamics for the right hand. It can also depend on the instrument, room, and mallets.
- **Don't hurt your back**
  - When you need to use the shaft of the mallets on the edges of the bars, try to avoid simply bending at the waist.
  - Instead, take a step back so that one foot is behind you and bend your knees to get lower.
  - This will help you maintain a good posture while avoiding back pain that may come from spending time bending over the instrument.
- **Have fun with the melodies**
  - Make sure that the melodies have some direction and groove. Remember that they're always going somewhere.
  - When you decide how to phrase the melody, support that phrasing with the accompaniment.
  - Keeping it underneath, have the accompaniment in the right hand gently rise and fall with that of the melodic voice in the left hand.

Mallets Used: Malletech - Overly soft CN9, 2-MB8, MB13

Eastern Promises

for Zachary Paul Burritt

Michael Burritt

4

Supplemental Exercises III

These exercises are inspired by Michael Burritt's *Eastern Promises.* Aim for a range in tempo of 90 to 150 for the quarter note.

Matthew Curlee
Nocturne

Equal parts performer, composer, and educator, Matt Curlee (www.mattcurlee.com) has served on the faculty of the department of music theory at the Eastman School of Music since 2007. As both an advocate for, and avid practitioner of improvisational music, Curlee has a particular interest in ear-brain interactions and the intuitive processes that unify composition, improvisation, and performance. This area of research has fed directly into his work at Eastman, where he has designed an advanced skills curriculum for the undergraduate honors program. In a forthcoming book, his approach to advanced cognition-based aural musicianship training will be offered in a format for individual use by those who wish to build their flexibility and fluency beyond the scope of practice generally covered in a collegiate music program.

As a composer, Curlee's recent work has focused on the interplay between modern theoretical and experimental physics and the arts (www.h-universe.org). Notable among these projects, Histories is a continuing set of collaborations between composer Matt Curlee and physicist Regina Demina, exploring the fundamental narratives, at various scales, that form the fabric of reality. Current projects and commissions include new music for the Eastman Percussion Ensemble's 2016-17 season, for the Strong National Museum of Play, a chamber concerto for 'cello, a suite of student pieces for marimba, a song cycle featuring the poetry of A.E. Housman, and a set of arrangements celebrating the 40th anniversary of the release of Stevie Wonder's Songs in the Key of Life.

A native of Greensboro, North Carolina, Matt has lived in Rochester, New York since 1994, and holds two degrees and a performer's certificate from Eastman.

- *Tempo dictates technique*
  - *Nocturne* has a broad range of tempos.
  - At the slower tempo of 108, you will find that there is an abundance of single alternating strokes.
  - As you get closer to 120, they will turn into double lateral strokes.
  - This is an excellent example of the single alternating speed limit. No matter what stroke type is used, strive for a smooth sound throughout.
- *Small Intervals*
  - Small intervals can be as tricky as large ones.
  - Make sure that you avoid rotating the hand so that the palm is facing down.
  - Keep the hand vertical and use the index finger and thumb to pull the inside mallet towards the outside.
- *Don't be static*
  - Don't let every note sound the same!
  - There are note groups of 3, 4, and 5 throughout the piece.
  - Find subtle ways of phrasing these groupings so that the audience can feel them with you.
  - You don't want it to sound like an endless string of eighth notes.
- *Dynamics*
  - For the most part, *Nocturne* uses a softer dynamic range. Use this range to it's potential.
  - Since there is a level that may border on too loud, explore the softer levels and expand down.
  - Unless otherwise notated, make sure that your crescendos and decrescendos are smooth.
  - Avoid sudden jumps in dynamic with the exception of subito dynamic shifts.

Mallets Used: Malletech - CH4, 2-CH8, CN9

for Mark Boseman

Nocturne
for marimba

Matt Curlee (2016)

Supplemental Exercises IV

These exercises are inspired by Matthew Curlee's *Nocturne*. Aim for a range in tempo of 60 to 80 for the quarter note and 75 to 110 for the dotted quarter note.

Elliot Cole

Evensong

Elliot Cole (*1984) is a composer, performer, and "charismatic contemporary bard" (NY Times). His book of bowed vibraphone quartets, Postludes, evokes "sparkling icicles of sound" (Rolling Stone), and is a new staple of percussion repertoire, having been performed by over 140 ensembles all over the world, including all major American music schools, So Percussion, Blow Up Roma, and Amadinda. He has sung hisHanuman's Leap, a bardic epic for voices and drums, in 15 cities, and will record it with Grammy-winning vocal group Roomful of Teeth in 2016 after two sold-out shows at the Park Avenue Armory. Oracle Hysterical, his creative friendship (part band, part book club) with Brad and Doug Balliett and Majel Connery has produced genre-bending collaborations with the A Far Cry, Chicago Composers Orchestra, New Vintage Baroque, Metropolis Ensemble, MATA, the Berkshire Fringe Festival, and the Lucerne Festival Academy, where they were Spotlight Artists in 2011. He lives in Jersey City and is a faculty member of the Manhattan School of Music, The New School, Juilliard Evening Division, and is Program Director of Musicambia at Sing Sing correctional facility.

Learn more at www.elliotcole.com

- *Soft Mallets*
  - You want to create the illusion of sustain without excessive contact noise.
  - If you don't have a set of soft mallets, experiment with beating spots and angles using the mallets that you do have. Sometimes you have to make do with what you have.
- *Learn the piece with block chords instead of rolls*
  - Pick a note value (i.e. sixteenth or sixteenth note triplets) and practice the piece as block chords.
  - It will help you keep proper time and let you practice your shifts.
  - When you're comfortable, double the note value and offset the hands.
  - When that becomes comfortable, switch to a traditional roll.
- *Make it smooth*
  - Avoid locking your wrists and using your arms. Smooth motions will create smooth sounds.
  - Try to avoid sudden jumps in roll speed. Instead, adjust gradually depending on where you are on the instrument along with an important harmony or climax.
  - Leading with the left hand will give the impression that all four voices are moving together, rather than the upper voices moving first.
- *Balance*
  - When you need to bring a line out, have that hand play a little louder than the other.
  - At the beginning, the left needs to play louder to bring out the moving line.
  - Towards the end, the right hand needs to be slightly louder.
  - Be aware of what you want the audience to hear and bring it out of the texture.

Mallets Used: Malletech - LS1, 2-LS5, LS10

Evensong

Elliot Cole

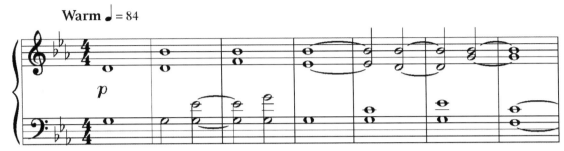

bring out inner line

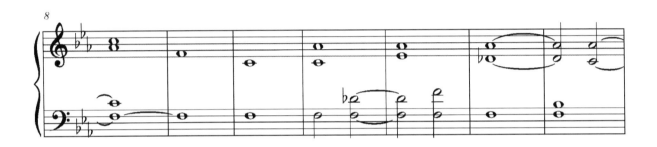

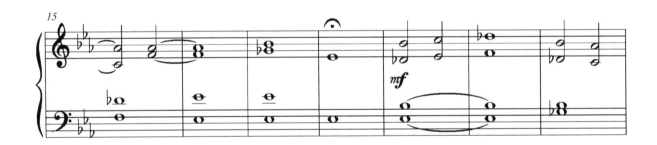

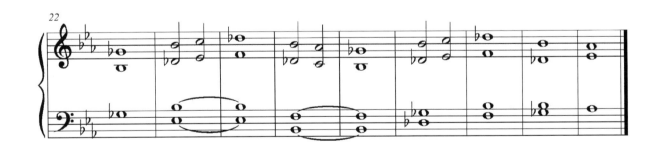

Supplemental Exercises V

These exercises are inspired by Elliot Cole's's *Evensong*. Aim for a range in tempo of 60 to 100 for the quarter note.

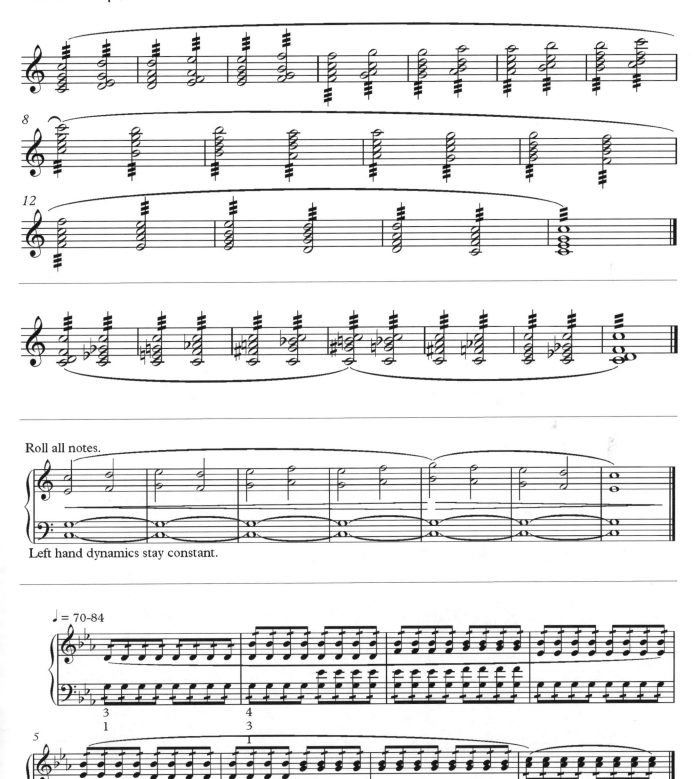

Roll all notes.

Left hand dynamics stay constant.

$\quad$ = 70–84

8

Music: Volume II

Robert Honstein *Independent*

Blake Tyson *Night Light*

Ivan Trevino *Float Like a Butterfly*

Jennifer Bellor *Afterglow*

Baljinder Sekhon *Intervals & Angles*

Robert Honstein

Independent

Robert Honstein is a Boston-based composer of orchestral, chamber, and vocal music. His works have been performed throughout the world by leading ensembles including the Cabrillo Festival Orchestra, the Albany Symphony Orchestra, Eighth Blackbird, Ensemble ACJW, Ensemble Dal Niente, the Mivos quartet, the Del Sol Quartet, Present Music, the Pittsburgh New Music Ensemble, and the Correction Line Ensemble, of which he is a founding member. He has received an Aaron Copland Award, multiple ASCAP awards and honors from SCI, Carnegie Hall, and New Music USA. He has also received residencies at the MacDowell Colony, Copland House, the Bang on a Can Summer Institute, and the Tanglewood Music Center. Robert co- produces Fast Forward Austin, an annual marathon new music concert in Austin, TX and is a founding member of the New York based composer collective Sleeping Giant. His debut album 'RE: You' was released by New Focus Recordings in 2014 and his second album, a collaboration with the Sebastians, was released on Soundspells Productions in 2015. In 2016 Cedille records released Sleeping Giant's collaboration with Eighth Blackbird, 'Hand Eye', to critical acclaim.

Learn more at http://www.roberthonstein.com

- **Correct Technique**
  - Make sure that the single independent strokes are smooth and don't have any excessive movement in the unused mallet.
  - Avoid using the forearms to play the stroke.
  - Too much vertical motion in the other mallet means that there is too much forward motion in the wrist. If the other mallet moves up and/or over the hand, there is too much rotation.
- **Polyrhythms**
  - The A section features polyrhythms that frequently shift in note value between the hands.
  - Get comfortable with the composite rhythms as well as shifting from one to the next on a practice pad or drum.
  - This will help you get comfortable with the polyrhythms without the notes getting in the way.
- **Practice your scales**
  - The B section of the piece features quite a bit of scale material
  - Practice scales in all 12 keys using mallets 2 and 3.
  - Be mindful of the quality of sound if you are moving from off center of the natural manual to the edges of the accidental manual.
  - Don't play with static dynamics. Add crescendos and decrescendos to practice phrasing.
- **Know the melody**
  - In m.m 46-50, there is a statement of the melody. As the piece progresses, the music around it becomes more complicated.
  - Make sure that the melody is always present no matter what is happening around it.
  - 99/100 times, the difficult and complicated part is less important in the musical hierarchy.

Mallets Used: Malletech - Overly soft CN9, 2-MB8, MB13

for Mark Boseman
Independent

Robert Honstein (2016)

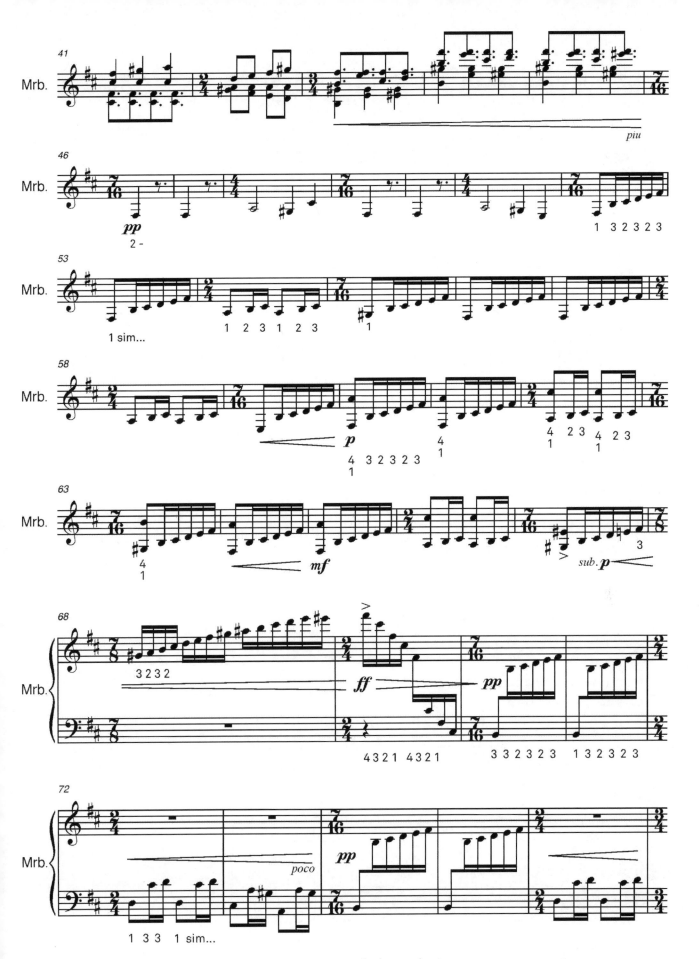

Independent
© 2016 Robert Honstein

** staccato = dead stroke

Independent
© 2016 Robert Honstein

Supplemental Exercises VI

These exercises are inspired by Robert Honstein's *Independent*. Aim for a range in tempo of 75 to 115 for the quarter note and 60 to 100 for the dotted quarter note.

Blake Tyson

Night Light

Blake Tyson's compositions are performed in concert halls around the world, and his own performances have taken him to five continents and over thirty states. He has performed in Egypt at the Ministry of Culture in Cairo and at the Library of Alexandria, at international festivals in South Africa and South America, at the Beijing Central Conservatory, in Norway as part of the European Cultural Capital celebrations, and at the Percussive Arts Society International Convention. He has also performed at events throughout the United States, including numerous Days of Percussion, the Northwest Percussion Festival, and the Leigh Howard Stevens Summer Marimba Seminar. He has presented clinics and masterclasses at many universities both in the United States and abroad. Blake is a concert artist and clinician for the Zildjian Company and with Malletech, where he has his own line of signature mallets.

Blake Tyson holds a Doctor of Musical Arts from the Eastman School of Music. While at Eastman, he was also awarded the prestigious Performer's Certificate. He holds a Master of Music degree from Kent State University and the degree of Bachelor of Music in Performance from the University of Alabama. His teachers include Marjorie Engle, Peggy Benkeser, Larry Mathis, Michael Burritt, Halim El-Dabh, and John Beck. Since 2001, Blake has been a member of the faculty of the University of Central Arkansas.

Learn more at http://www.blaketyson.com

- **Correct Technique**
  - *Night Light* relies heavily on the double lateral stroke.
  - Remember that it is a rotation of the wrist that will produce two notes out of a single motion.
  - Avoid letting your arms get involved by locking up the wrist and using a "flam" motion.
- **Keep your wrists aligned**
  - Starting in measure 3, you will need to navigate between a G natural and A flat with your right hand.
  - Make sure that there are no unnatural bends in your wrist.
  - Swing your elbow out so that your forearm is parallel to your body in order to keep the wrist and forearm in alignment.
- **Don't lose the melody**
  - With the high amount of rhythmic activity, it can be easy for the melody to take a back seat to the busier rhythms.
  - For example, in measure 15 the number 4 mallet has the melody.
  - Listen for the quarter and half note melody rather than a succession of sixteenth notes.
  - In order to practice it, pull the melody out of the texture and work on phrasing. When you decide on how to treat the melody, put it back in the original texture.
- **Support the melody**
  - 99/100 times, the more active or complicated part isn't the more important part.
  - In a busy texture such as this, the accompaniment can easily overshadow the more important melodies.
  - Try to keep the accompaniment light and shape it in a way that can follow the phrasing of the melody without surpassing it.

Mallets Used: Malletech - Overly soft CN9,
2-MB8, MB13

Night Light

for Mark Boseman

Blake Tyson

68

2

4

8

Supplemental Exercises VII

These exercises are inspired by Blake Tyson's *Night Light*. Aim for a range in tempo of 70 to 120 for the quarter note.

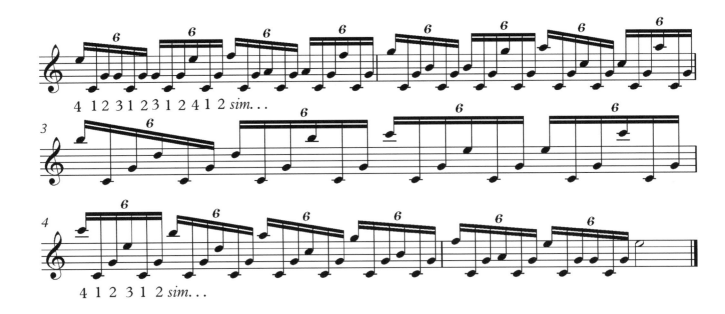

Night Light: Stepping into the forest, it seems almost pitch black, but the further you walk, the more you notice silvery starlight flickering through the leaves. At a clearing you look up to floating, wispy clouds glowing in the light of the moon. The forest seems brighter than ever as you bound through the trees toward the river. The sparkling light of the night reflects off its shimmering surface. You rest on the bank as fireflies glow all around you.

Ivan Trevino

Float Like a Butterfly

(b.1983) Ivan Trevino is an award-winning composer, percussionist, and rock drummer currently living in Austin, TX. As a composer, Ivan's music is regularly performed around the world and has become standard repertoire in the field of percussion. He is a multi-award winning recipient of the Percussive Arts Society's International Composition Contest and has been commissioned by some of the world's leading performers and universities in the field of percussion.

Ivan is also a songwriter and rock drummer with Break of Reality, an international touring cello and percussion quartet. As a member of Break of Reality, Ivan has headlined concerts across North America, South America, and Asia and was named a music ambassador for the U.S. State Department in 2015. Ivan's drumming and songwriting with Break of Reality have been heard on NPR, PBS, Huffington Post and Yahoo Music.

In addition to composing and performing, Ivan is also an active educator. He is a member of the percussion faculty at Baylor University and frequently attends colleges and universities as a guest artist and lecturer. He is currently an artist / clinician for Malletech Instruments and Mallets, Zildjian Cymbals, and Evans Drumheads. In 2014, Malletech collaborated with Ivan to design his signature marimba mallets, which are now distributed to percussionists around the world.

Ivan's sheet music is available at IvanDrums.com, Steve Weiss Music and Lone Star Percussion.

- **Correct Technique**
  - *Float Like a Butterfly* relies on the single alternating stroke for the introduction and conclusion.
  - Make sure that you are using a bouncing motion between the mallets, which is an extension of the single independent stroke.

- **Separate Hands**
  - The piece will introduce multiple themes and layer them on top of one another.
  - A good way to practice is by learning the music in each hand separately, then putting them together.
  - This will make the piece more manageable to learn.

- **Infuse your own dynamics**
  - A common thread of Ivan's music is the notable absence of heavy dynamic markings. This is intentional.
  - Look at this as an opportunity to make the piece unique to you.
  - Make each note have a clear direction so that it will be continually moving towards the moments that are special to you.
  - Listen for the top voice in the opening phrase. That is the major theme.
  - Listen for ways that this theme is developed throughout the piece. Find ways to not only make it noticeable, but to also vary it throughout the piece.

Mallets Used: Malletech - Overly soft CN9, 2-MB8, MB13

solo marimba
4.3 octave

float like a butterfly

for solo marimba
Dedicated to Dr. Mark Boseman. In memory of Muhammad Ali.

Ivan Trevino

float like a butterfly

similar to beginning, this time open to improvisation within style of section...
player can take liberties with length of phrases.

Supplemental Exercises VIII

These exercises are inspired by Ivan Trevino's *Float Like a Butterfly*. Aim for a range in tempo of 75 to 130 for the quarter note.

Conitnue in all 12 keys

Jennifer Bellor
Afterglow

Las Vegas-based composer Jennifer Bellor blends contemporary jazz, classical, and rock styles, and enjoys collaborating will jazz and classical musicians, dancers, poets, filmmakers, and visual artists. Her works have been performed by national and international organizations such as Washington National Opera, Lviv Philharmonic, Seattle Women's Jazz Orchestra, ACO Jazz Composers Orchestra Institute readings in New York City, North American Saxophone Alliance Conference, Aspen Music Festival, June in Buffalo, Eastman New Jazz Ensemble, Eastman Wind Ensemble, Eastman Saxophone Project, UNLV Wind Symphony, Nazareth College Wind Symphony, California State University East Bay Wind Orchestra, UNLV Jazz Ensemble, Florida State University Festival of New Music, Hildegard Festival, Ritsos Project in Greece, A/ Tonal Ensemble, and many others in the United States and abroad.

Jennifer's debut album Stay released August 10th, 2016 blends jazz, classical and rock styles, featuring classical and jazz artists affiliated with Eastman School of Music and University of Nevada, Las Vegas. Additionally, her track Chase the Stars features Las Vegas-based rapper Rasar Amani. For more information on her album, please visit the Discography page on her website www.jenniferbellor.com

Jennifer earned a PhD in music composition at Eastman School of Music, a Master of Music degree in composition at Syracuse University, and a Bachelor of Arts degree in music at Cornell University. Her primary composition teachers included David Liptak, Bob Morris, Andrew Waggoner, Sally Lamb-McCune, and Steven Stucky. She is currently Visiting Lecturer at University of Nevada, Las Vegas, where she teaches courses in music composition and theory.

- *Independence*
  - The independent rolls can create problems when you have to use the other hand.
  - To practice, start rolling at a comfortable interval (i.e. a 5th) and practice the rhythms on single note.
  - Taking away the need to play the right notes can help separate the hands more easily.
- *Keep it smooth*
  - While working on your independent rolls, be mindful of the quality of the rolls.
  - Make sure that each roll stroke are even with each other in both rhythms and dynamic.
  - If fatigue sets in, and it probably will at some point, try to relax and play a little softer.
  - Build your endurance with good habits rather than instinctually tensing up and "muscling it out".
- *Know the role (roll)*
  - In *Afterglow*, the independent rolls often play an accompaniment role to the melodic material.
  - Make sure that you don't overplay them.
  - Try playing the beginning of each roll slightly louder only to immediately get softer.
  - Also keep in mind that in the lower range, the roll speed will be slower. Don't work harder than you need to by playing the rolls too fast.
- *Keep the flow going*
  - There are some beautiful moments that fall outside of the independent roll sections.
  - Make sure that they don't sound too static or overly rhythmic.
  - Have some groove when it's needed along with some beautiful flowing lines.
  - Remember that the music is always going somewhere. It's never stationary.

Mallets Used: Malletech - CH4, 2-CH8, CN9

AFTERGLOW

Jennifer K. Bellor

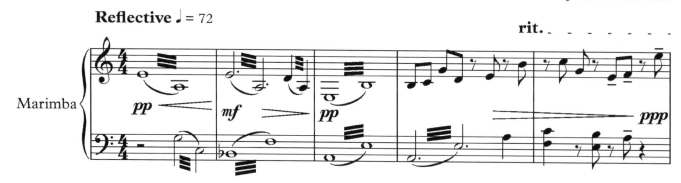

Supplemental Exercises IX

These exercises are inspired by Jennifer Bellor's *Afterglow*. Aim for a range in tempo of 60 to 100 for the quarter note.

Baljinder Sekhon
Intervals & Angles

"Clearly knowing the power of sonority" (Philadelphia Inquirer), the music of Baljinder Sekhon has been presented in over 400 concerts in twenty countries. Performances of Sekhon's music have included those at prestigious venues such as Carnegie Hall and the Seoul Arts Center. Ten commercial recordings of his works have been released, and his compositions have received performances and recordings by prominent ensembles and performers, such as the Albany Symphony, Cabrillo Festival Orchestra, line upon line, Los Angeles Percussion Quartet, Thailand Philharmonic Orchestra, and the Eastman Wind Ensemble. Additional platforms for the performance of Sekhon's music have included the National Orchestra Institute, National Saxophone Alliance Conference, The Jerome L. Greene Performance Space, the Paris Conservatory, MATA's Interval Series, New World Symphony's Musician Forum Series, the World Saxophone Congress, International Viola Congress, Juventas New Music Ensemble, the Percussive Arts Society International Convention, Bang On a Can Festival, Stallenbosch International Chamber Music Festival, and a full concert of his works at John Zorn's contemporary art space The Stone. Sekhon serves as Assistant Professor of Composition at the University of South Florida and holds the PhD and MA from the Eastman School of Music where he is a three-time recipient of the Howard Hanson Orchestral prize. His numerous appearances as a percussionist include those at the L.A. Philharmonic's Green Umbrella Series in Walt Disney Hall, Festival Spazio Musica in Cagliari, Italy, and at the Bang On a Can Marathon in New York City.

Learn more at http://www.sekhonmusic.com

- **Single note independent rolls**
  - There are many times where your body position can make the rolls physically difficult.
  - Try to keep your forearm, wrist, and hands in a natural alignment to avoid excessive angles with your wrists.
  - You'll want to have as much leverage as possible to comfortably play the independent rolls.
  - Depending on which hand is playing, position one mallet slightly off center and the other at the lower edge.
  - This will give the mallets some space so that you won't have to roll with an extremely small interval.
- **Learn it without the rolls**
  - At first, take the rolls out completely.
  - Replace them with dead strokes that last for the duration of the roll and learn the correct notes along with when and where to shift.
  - As you get more comfortable, start replacing the dead strokes with independent rolls.
- **Don't over play the rolls**
  - Instinct can tell us to play the rolls in a way that they are the focus of the listener's ear.
  - Make sure that you don't take this concept too far so that you lose control of the roll.
  - Early on, take a little off of the rolls and build your strength.
- **Smooth rolls**
  - In the single line melodies, try to make the shift from one roll to the next as smooth as possible.
  - In most cases, all that is required is simply moving the arm from one place to the next.
  - Avoid adding extra tension or automatically altering the roll speed that creates a momentary surge in the roll.
  - Try playing just those lines with two mallets and then mimicking the phrasing with independent rolls.

Mallets Used: Malletech - 2 LS1, 2 LS10

Intervals & Angles
an etude for one-handed rolls

Solo Marimba

Baljinder Singh Sekhon, II

Intervals & Angles

Intervals & Angles

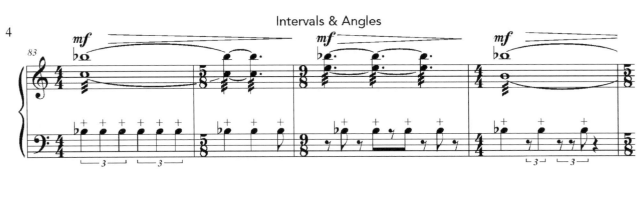

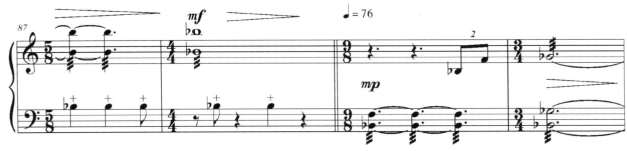

Supplemental Exercises X

These exercises are inspired by Baljinder Sekhon's. Aim for a range in tempo of 60 to 90 for the quarter note. All rolls should be played as independent rolls.

Intervals & Angles is an etude for solo marimba designed to give the performer an opportunity to develop the one-handed-roll technique in both hands, at every interval, and every angle possible. In order to achieve this, a twelve-tone row was employed as an oblique counterpoint line to a constant pitch that generates a series of dyads consisting of all diatonic intervals within an octave. This series is presented in three different transpositions that allows for the three variations of mallet angles in one hand (flat, inward, and outward). Another aspect of this work is the interaction between the two hands: the piece requires the performer to roll with one hand while playing melodic material with the other and roll with one hand while playing a constant pitch with the other. In the middle section, the two hands work together in a variety of coinciding and opposing angles to provide an opportunity to develop simultaneous one-handed rolls. In total, this work will give the student the opportunity to develop technique, learn to perform in a variety of meters, and provide a basic understanding of twelve-tone music. In addition to developing the technique, the student is encouraged to analyze the piece finding the three row transformations within the piece.

Thanks.

I sincerely hope that you have enjoyed using this book as much as I have enjoyed writing it. From the beginning, this has never been about writing something better than what had been written before. It is simply the method in which I learned and the way that I have taught my students over the years. Sometimes hearing the same material in a slightly different way is enough to make it resonate. It is also my hope that the hard work of not only myself, but that of the incredibly talented composers put into this project will be evident. As you use this book please keep in mind that it is a completely self published and self promoted work. If you have enjoyed using it, please share your experiences and thoughts on both social media and in the real world. However, please refrain from using copying or file sharing to express your enthusiasm for this book. Above all else, I hope that you will take whatever you have learned and run with it. It is meant to be a good starting point and a firm foundation and it's up to you to continually challenge yourself and take this as far as you want to go.

Sincerely,

Made in the USA
Middletown, DE
17 November 2017